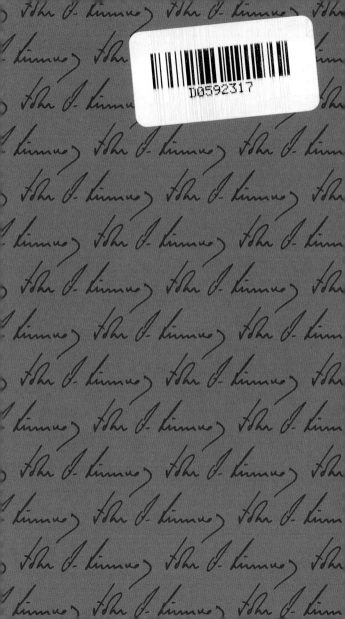

A SHORT BIOGRAPHY OF JOHN F. KENNEDY

A SHORT BIOGRAPHY OF
John F. Kennedy

Mim Harrison

BENNA BOOKS

Carlisle, Massachusetts

A Short Biography of John F. Kennedy

Series Editor: Susan DeLand
Written by: Mim Harrison

Copyright © 2017 Applewood Books, Inc.

978-1-944038-29-8

Front cover: *John F. Kennedy, 35th President of the Unites States, 1961–1963,*
1970, Aaron Shikler, Oil on canvas
35.97 cm x 53.09 cm
White House Collection / White House Historical Association
Back cover: *President John F. Kennedy Sails Aboard Yacht "Manitou,"*
August 12, 1962, Robert Knudsen, White House Photographer
Negative (color: 4 x 5 inches)
Courtesy of the John F. Kennedy Library and Museum, Boston, MA
KN-C23216

Published by Benna Books
an imprint of Applewood Books
Carlisle, Massachusetts

To request a free copy of our current catalog
featuring our best-selling books, write to:
Applewood Books
P.O. Box 27
Carlisle, MA 01741
Or visit us on the web at: www.awb.com

10 9 8 7 6 5 4 3 2 1
MANUFACTURED IN THE UNITED STATES OF AMERICA

JOHN F. KENNEDY WAS AMERICA'S thirty-fifth president and the first president to be born in the twentieth century. Time-Life publisher Henry Luce christened it the "American Century," and JFK's presidency was a key element in making it so.

John Fitzgerald Kennedy—quickly known as Jack—was born on May 29, 1917, in the Boston suburb of Brookline. He was the second of nine children in an Irish Catholic family that was large in size and larger than life in the dynastic role it would assume in America's history, even to the present day.

Being an Irish Catholic in Boston at the turn of the twentieth century was, for the most part, not an enviable situation. The huge wave of immigrants from Ireland met with discrimination, as seen in classified ads that advised: "No Irish need apply." Due to this bias many took unskilled blue-collar jobs, though in Boston they were well skilled in politics.

Jack's family, however, was above this fray. His mother, Rose, was considered part of the genteel "lace curtain Irish." Her father, John Francis Fitzgerald—popularly known as "Honey Fitz"—was a striving congressman who also became Boston's mayor. He even ran for the U.S. Senate against Henry Cabot Lodge, one of the Boston Brahmins—a term coined by Oliver Wendell Holmes in one of his novels published in the nineteenth century. With a nod to the caste system of India, this term described wealthy, elite Bostonians who could often trace their lineage back to the Puritans. In other words, they were "white Anglo-Saxon Protestants," known as WASPs. They were here first, and they made it clear immigrants were not welcome. Even more significant, Joseph P. Kennedy, Jack's father, was shrewd, competitive, and ruthlessly ambitious. A cagey stock trader, he was a millionaire by 1926 and went on to benefit greatly from investing in Hollywood films and starting a liquor import business, just as Prohibition was ending. Joe and Rose, both Bostonians, had known each other since childhood and were dating by high school (to Honey Fitz's chagrin). They married in October 1914. She was twenty-four; he was twenty-five.

Joe exhorted his children to do their absolute best, instilling a certain rivalry and competitiveness among them. Even so, it was a family that was loyal to one another. In that sense, it was indeed a clan: four boys—Joseph Jr., John, Robert, and Edward—and five girls—Rosemary, Kathleen (whom Jack was particularly close to), Eunice, Pat, and Jean.

"If your family is a success you're a

In one verbal sparring with Lodge, Fitzgerald reminded him that (almost) all Americans had been immigrants: "It's only a difference of a few ships."

success," Joe believed, and he was determined that his children would triumph in the largest possible way. The power, Joe Kennedy believed, lay in politics. Rose, having grown up in a political household, was very much his partner in that regard, and she would be one of her son Jack's earliest and most steadfast campaigners around Boston.

As privileged as Jack was, he was not immune from illness. When he was two, he contracted scarlet fever and was quarantined away from his home for weeks. It would be the beginning of a growing number of illnesses and conditions—often serious, but frequently without definitive diagnoses—that would plague him all his life. The most chronic of his illnesses were gastrointestinal issues and debilitating back pain. Years later, Jack would be diagnosed with Addison's disease, which affects the adrenal glands.

But illness did one good thing for young Jack: it made him a reader. At an early age, he was reading Rudyard Kipling, Harriet

Beecher Stowe, James Fenimore Cooper, and Robert Louis Stevenson. (Stevenson had been another "sick little boy," as Jackie Kennedy once described her husband's childhood.) By the time he got to Choate, the elite boys' boarding school near New Haven, Jack was reading Churchill's *The World Crisis* during stays in the hospital.

Another favorite book of his was *King Arthur and the Round Table,* with the knights' castle city of Camelot.

Like the young and severely asthmatic Teddy Roosevelt, Jack refused to let his health issues define or impede him. And just like Roosevelt, he went west—albeit for just a few months in the summer of 1936—and worked as a ranch hand in Arizona.

Jack's headmaster at Choate summed up his academic performance this way: "Rules bother him a bit." Jack was not like his star older brother, Joe Jr. —and he would be the first one to say so. He did, however, excel in English class, preferring the poetry of Robert Frost to physics.

Although Kennedy is closely connected with Harvard, where he earned his bachelor's degree in 1940, he initially went to

Princeton because his close friends from Choate had gone there. But he transferred to Harvard shortly afterward. Part of the impetus was the desire to play football, even though his was hardly the classic football build: his six-foot frame often carried as little as 135 pounds.

Jack told his freshman adviser at Harvard that he wanted to "work in government." He proceeded to run in his first election, representing his freshman class—and lost.

But he won friends easily, starting at Choate and continuing through his life—a combination of charm, wit, and his determination to, as he told one friend in November 1963, "live each day like it's your last." The friends he made at school, and later in the navy and during his early days in Congress, would remain his close friends even after he became president. In fact, his oldest friend from Choate, Lem Billings, knew that there was always a room for him at the White House.

Jack was never an all-A student, but

he had an exceptional mind. His spelling may have been spotty, but his vocabulary was robust. He kept notebooks of quotations by historic personages—Thomas Jefferson, Thomas Paine—that he wished to remember. It was a habit he would long continue.

Jack Kennedy was a thinker and a questioner.

"Change is the law of life. And those who look only to the past or the present are certain to miss the future."

In January 1938, President Franklin Roosevelt appointed Joseph P. Kennedy as U.S. ambassador to Great Britain. Jack joined his family in England in the spring of 1939. At age twenty-two, he became an unofficial political reporter for his father, traveling to the Soviet Union, the Middle East, and Europe to gauge the political climate. Just days before Hitler invaded Poland on September 1, Jack was shuttling between Prague and Germany.

Traveling abroad at that time was not

commonplace. A worldview was primarily the province of the privileged, and within that small world Jack had an entrée few would attain because of his father's position. In London, he sat in Parliament and listened as Winston Churchill importuned the English people to recognize the unassailable danger of Hitler. For the most part, they turned a deaf ear.

But Jack did not, and his Harvard thesis became a commentary on why he felt Britain was ill prepared for war. The thesis became a book, *Why England Slept,* which became a best seller.

After Harvard, Jack headed to Stanford and audited courses in political science and economics. Then he took a six-week tour of South America. At age twenty-four, he had seen more of the world than most of his generation ever would. And he would soon see more still: the South Pacific.

In what was perhaps a harbinger of the call JFK would so memorably make in 1961 to "ask what you can do for your country," he answered that call himself in

1941. Jack had to pull (his father's) strings to get drafted to fight in World War II because of his questionable health. He made it into the navy and in 1943 answered another call, for volunteers to skipper patrol torpedo—or PT—boats.

PT boats carried both torpedoes and machine guns.

Depending on whom you asked, these were either the best or the worst boats to deploy on stealth nighttime missions to cripple the enemy's supply convoy for its soldiers. The first requirement for those who volunteered was that they be courageous. They also had to be young, single, and healthy. Jack figured three out of four should be sufficient, and with a few pulled strings it was.

Jack was the skipper of PT-109. Around 2:30 a.m. on August 2, 1943, he and his crew were in the waters around the Solomon Islands, which the Allies had recaptured from Japan, when a Japanese destroyer slammed into the boat. Two of the crew were killed instantly. Kennedy and some of the other less injured men rescued the rest. They languished in the boat until around 1:00 p.m., when Kennedy ordered them to abandon the ship, which was in danger of sinking, and head toward the nearest island, which had the improbable name of Plum Pudding. One crew member, severely burned, couldn't make it under his own steam. Kennedy, who had taken competitive swimming at Choate and Harvard, swam him to safety. The three-and-a-half-mile swim took nearly four hours. It would then be another six days before the exhausted crew would be rescued by other PT boats, helped in large part by native islanders who were Allied scouts and saved them from being killed or captured by the enemy.

Jack towed the injured crewman by a belt that he held between his teeth as he swam for four hours.

Instead of being shipped back to the States after that, which was his prerogative, Kennedy insisted on skippering another PT boat. He volunteered for many missions, including a rescue of scores of Marines. Kennedy quit his PT boat service only when the naval doctor had the emaciated-looking skipper relieved of his command.

Jack's return to the States came with a Navy and Marine Corps Medal for heroism, a Purple Heart, and malaria he'd contracted in the South Pacific. He underwent surgery for his chronic back pain with little success.

In August 1944, the first of many Kennedy family tragedies struck: Joe Jr., a navy flier, was killed during a high-risk combat mission in Europe. Jack was recovering from back surgery at the Chelsea Naval Hospital near Boston when he got the devastating news. It was Joe—the model student, the son who hewed to a more traditional path—whom his father had planned would be president. Now, as a grieving Jack told a friend, "the burden falls on me."

But clearly Jack had the passion for politics. His friend Charles Bartlett recalled him saying, after a brief stint as a stringer for a Chicago newspaper, "You can't make changes [as a journalist]. There's no impact. I'm going to go into politics and see if you can really do anything."

Over the years, Kennedy would periodically have to resort to using crutches because of the debilitating pain in his back, but rarely in public.

World War II ended in September 1945, and, at age twenty-eight, Jack ran as a Democrat for U.S. representative in his home district in Boston and won. He served three terms, making the Cold War his cause and going to Berlin in 1948 to witness a city literally divided into democratic and Communist rule. He and Congressman Richard Nixon were cordial colleagues despite party difference.

In 1952, Jack ran for the Senate against Henry Cabot Lodge Jr. and did what his grandfather Honey Fitz had not been able to do with Lodge's grandfather: Kennedy beat him. The next year Jack married the woman his friend Bartlett had introduced him to at a dinner party, Jacqueline Lee Bouvier. Her double-take good looks were part of the attraction, but so were her wit and intellect. The same could be said of Jackie's feelings toward him. A tactic of Jack's courtship was giving Jackie copies of his favorite books: *Young Melbourne,* by Lord David Cecil, and *Pilgrim's Way,* by John Buchan.

More than nine hundred guests attended Jack and Jackie's September wedding reception at Hammersmith Farm, the oceanfront estate of Jackie's mother in Newport, Rhode Island.

His back pain worsened the following year, driving him to undergo spinal surgery that left him comatose. Jackie prayed for him; so did his congressional colleague Richard Nixon. During his recovery, the bedridden Jack worked on the book that would win him the Pulitzer Prize: *Profiles in Courage,* a collection of short biographies of eight U.S. senators who in Kennedy's view demonstrated extraordinary political courage and integrity.

At the Democratic National Convention in Chicago in 1956, Jack made a play to be Adlai Stevenson's vice-presidential candidate. Although he lost the bid, he scored an important victory nonetheless: he won the attention of the American people, who were watching it all on TV.

"Wisdom requires the long view."

On January 2, 1960, now-Senator Jack Kennedy was getting a haircut. He was also dictating to his secretary an announcement he would make a few hours

He would be the first Roman Catholic to run for president and, at forty-three, the youngest candidate.

later: John F. Kennedy was running for president of the United States on the Democratic ticket.

Richard Nixon was his Republican opponent. Many believe that one of the determining factors in Kennedy's winning the presidency was the series of televised debates the two held starting on September 26. Though routine now, in 1960 television was still a relatively new medium, and had never before been used to broadcast a presidential debate. It was also, of course, a highly visual medium. The telegenic Kennedy—youthful, appearing to be fit and vigorous—easily eclipsed the older, ponderous Nixon.

Tuesday, November 8, was election day. By the end of the night, the race was too close to call. By 3:00 a.m. it was still close but tilting toward Kennedy. JFK, who was watching the returns at the family's Hyannisport compound, went to bed before Nixon formally conceded.

The inaugural address that John F. Kennedy delivered on the bitterly cold day of

January 20, 1961, is to this day ranked as one of the finest speeches of the twentieth century. It was also, intentionally, short—just 1,347 words.

One scholar calls the inaugural address JFK's "philosophical autobiography." Its iconic phrases still resonate: "Let the word go forth…that the torch has been passed to a new generation of Americans…"; "Now the trumpet summons us again…"; and the most memorable of all, "Ask not what your country can do for you—ask what you can do for your country."

Kennedy's delivery was as masterful as his words, his voice strong, his cadence measured. But none of that had come naturally. With the help of a voice coach, Kennedy had disciplined himself during the campaign to speak more slowly than his lightning-quick mind worked, and to inject the proper inflection. What's more, he remembered both Lincoln and Churchill. He recalled the elegant, elegiac grace of Lincoln's Gettysburg Address, which he so admired. And he remembered

The final count was 303 electoral votes for Kennedy, 219 for Nixon, and a razor-thin win of popular votes for JFK.

Churchill. During the time he spent in England in 1939, JFK had not only heard what Churchill said but how he delivered it—the stentorian voice, the vivid language, the dramatic pacing. In the oratory of Kennedy can be heard echoes of both Lincoln ("In your hands, my fellow citizens, more than mine…") and Churchill ("We shall pay any price, bear any burden, meet any hardship…").

Although the inaugural address went through numerous revisions, the copy that Kennedy read from was pristine. But the new president did not read from it verbatim. As he spoke, he edited himself in more than thirty places. "Ask not what your country will do for you…" read the text. Kennedy deftly changed "will" to "can" and instantly created a clarion call for his countrymen.

"Let us never negotiate out of fear. But let us never fear to negotiate."

In 1961, the specter of Communism

loomed large. It would color every for-eign-policy decision JFK made, from sending American aid and advisers to Vietnam to personally visiting West Berlin and condemning the wall.

But Communist threats lay even clos-er—in Cuba, a mere ninety miles from south Florida. In 1959, Fidel Castro had taken over the country and declared it Communist. An airlift of fourteen thou-sand Cuban children from Havana to the United States, called Operation Pedro Pan, began in 1960 and continued well into JFK's presidency. (The writer Carlos Eire, one of those children, recalled be-ing allowed to bring only two changes of clothes and one book.)

The CIA planned to overthrow Castro using Cuban exiles it had been training in Guatemala since 1960. Months before JFK was elected, Castro knew about the training camps. Regardless, Kennedy ex-ecuted the plan in April 1961, deploying bombers on April 15, for an air strike. The planes were off course accomplishing

The Cold War between the U.S. and the Soviet Union consumed the country in the 1950s and 1960s. Fear of Communism—the "Red Scare"—reached near hysteria, fanned by Senator Joseph McCarthy.

little except to expose their painted-over identifications as American. The land strike two days later was even more disastrous. Castro repelled the CIA's fourteen hundred guerrillas who came ashore from the Bay of Pigs with twenty thousand troops and the Cuban air force. Most of the exiles were killed or captured. It took twenty months and $53 million worth of baby food and medicine that the U.S. gave Castro to set the survivors free.

Cuba, essentially a proxy for the Soviet Union, would continue to be a threat. In October 1962, U.S. intelligence learned that the Soviets were setting up nuclear missiles in Cuba. Kennedy assembled a small and clandestine group of advisers to determine the best response. Some said the U.S. should bomb the missile sites; others said not to bomb. Kennedy opted to hold off, concerned that an air strike might trigger the nuclear attack the U.S. was trying to avert. Instead, he placed a naval blockade around the island.

Then, on October 22, he gave a tele-

The Soviet Union was known formally as the Union of Soviet Socialist Republics, or U.S.S.R. It encompassed fifteen countries, Russia being the largest.

vised address to the nation, which knew nothing of the threat. Soviet Premier Nikita Khrushchev responded with two letters, the first more conciliatory than the second. In the end, the Soviets did remove their missiles, although they continued to build up their military stockpile. Nevertheless, the threat of nuclear destruction that the Cuban Missile Crisis posed had been contained.

To prevent the spread of Communism in Latin America, Kennedy created the Alliance for Progress. As an economic aid and development project, it came with strong underpinnings of democratic measures that would benefit all the people in the recipient countries—not just the wealthy. It met with limited success and was disbanded in 1973.

Kennedy had used the phrase "alliance for progress" in his inaugural address.

A far more successful program was the Peace Corps, another form of rebutting Communism—this one on a global scale. JFK established it just weeks into his presidency, on March 1, 1961, and it continues to this day. "The toughest job you'll ever love" was its slogan for the first thirty years.

Peace Corps volunteers embed themselves within their country of outreach, helping developing countries in various aspects of community life, from education and nutrition to agriculture and business. The first group of volunteers came to the White House on August 28 for a personal farewell from their president.

The Soviet incursion into Europe extended beyond its "republics." Russia also controlled East Berlin. Khrushchev had erected a wall right through Berlin in 1961, thereby preventing East Berliners from easily defecting to the West. On June 26, 1963, Kennedy traveled to West Berlin. He had a prepared speech, but perhaps the sight of the ignominious wall and its assault on democratic principles caused him to add something more immediate.

Harking back to the ancient Romans' proud statement of *"Civis Romanus sum"*—"I am a citizen of Rome"—he had

One member of the first wave of the Peace Corps recalled precisely why he signed up: because JFK had put forth the call to ask what he could do for his country.

a translator prepare a similar show of support and solidarity in German. *"Ich bin ein Berliner,"* Kennedy famously declared to a cheering crowd—"I am a Berliner in spirit."

While the Berlin Wall was a physical affront to freedom, a different kind of wall in the United States was creating barriers to equality. Segregation of African Americans was still very much a reality in the South, and discrimination against them—in housing and employment—was prevalent throughout the country. Civil rights would loom large in Kennedy's presidency.

He and his brother Bobby, now the attorney general of the U.S., had already won Martin Luther King Jr.'s release from jail in Atlanta shortly before the election. But there was much more needed. At the beginning, Kennedy used executive orders rather than legislation to move agendas forward. His Executive Order 10925 created the Committee on Equal Employment Opportunity and spawned the term "affirmative action."

Kennedy had it written out phonetically so he would pronounce it properly: *"Ish bin ein Bearleener."*

In the fall of 1962, a veteran of the air force named James Meredith tried for a fifth time to register to attend the University of Mississippi—"Ole Miss." He was met with a hostile white mob because he was black. Kennedy sent in thousands of federal troops, and Meredith started classes at Ole Miss.

Just as television had played a major role in JFK's election, so it did with the civil rights movement as well.

When young African Americans staged demonstrations in Birmingham, Alabama, in 1963 after Martin Luther King Jr.'s arrest on Good Friday, the cameras caught police dogs and high-pressure fire hoses being turned on the protesters. JFK again sent in federal troops while he expedited the draft of a comprehensive civil rights bill.

That summer, a similar incident occurred at the University of Alabama, when Governor George Wallace stood in the doorway barring two African Americans from entering an auditorium. Kennedy summoned the National Guard and then, in effect, summoned the American people in a televised address on June 11, 1963.

"There is no uncontroversial way to fulfill our constitutional pledge to establish justice and promote domestic tranquility, but we intend to fulfill those obligations because they are right."

Equality, he told his viewers, was not just a legal matter. It was "a moral issue... as old as the Scriptures." Eight days later he called on Congress to pass the civil rights legislation because "above all, it is right." The bill was making its way through Congress when JFK was assassinated. His successor, Lyndon Johnson, shepherded its passage on July 2, 1964.

To add to Kennedy's legacy, a few weeks before taking office, when he was considering issues to bring to the fore, he had scribbled on the front of an envelope in his nearly illegible handwriting, "space." The Soviets were already ahead of the U.S. with the launch of their Sputnik satellite in 1957 and their successful manned orbit of Earth in 1961.

JFK's civil rights message to Congress was on June 19. In 1865, June 19—quickly named Juneteenth—marked the final announcement, by Union troops in Texas, of the end of slavery.

Kennedy aimed even higher. On May 25, 1961, he announced that "this nation should commit itself to achieving the goal, before the decade is out, of landing a man on the moon."

On July 20, 1969, America landed not one but two men on the moon.

During the Kennedy years, Jacqueline Kennedy elevated the White House to a beacon for many of the world's artists, musicians, and writers. It was a physical transformation as well as a cultural one. Jackie renovated the interior of the White House, restoring the rooms' histories. Then she gave Americans a guided tour in their living rooms, in a televised special that aired on Valentine's Day, 1962.

More than 80 million viewers tuned in on their TVs to watch a tour of the renovated White House with the First Lady.

Jackie's poise and refinement made her a powerful unofficial ambassador for her husband. Fluent in French and in fashion, she managed to charm Khrushchev, and she won the hearts of the French people during an official visit with JFK to France in June 1961. He famously quipped, by way of introducing himself, "I am the man who accompanied Jacqueline Kennedy to Paris."

She was a devoted mother to their children—Caroline, just three when Kennedy took office, and John Jr., a mere two months. Like their mother, an avid horsewoman, both children had their own ponies—Caroline's famous Macaroni and John's Leprechaun. The ponies were part of a delightful menagerie that included Tom Kitten the cat, Zsa Zsa the rabbit, a canary named Robin, and at least five dogs. One of them, Pushinka, was a gift from Khrushchev.

Pushinka was the offspring of Stelka, one of the dogs that orbited in the Soviet spaceship.

The Kennedys' next child, Patrick Bouvier Kennedy, was born prematurely in August 1963 and died within two days. A heartbroken Jackie stayed out of the public eye for weeks. That November, though, she agreed to accompany her husband on an early reelection swing through Texas—San Antonio, Houston, Fort Worth, Dallas, and Austin.

At approximately 12:30 p.m. local time on Friday, November 22, the open-top convertible carrying President and Mrs. Kennedy drove past the Texas School Book Depository in Dallas, and gunfire made its deadly mark. Kennedy was shot first in the neck and then the head. The frantic attempt at Parkland Hospital to save him failed. Walter Cronkite, the CBS news anchor, told Americans, with "a clinched jaw" as he struggled to maintain his composure, the news they did not want to hear: "President Kennedy died at 1:00 p.m. Central Standard Time." Ted Sorensen, special counsel to the president, wrote in his memoir *Counselor,* "There was no chaos, no shrieking or wailing…just disbelief and grief…. I tried to force myself to think about the future—including my future—but could not." Lee Harvey Oswald, who worked at the depository, was almost immediately arrested. Two days later, as he was being moved to the county jail, a nightclub owner named Jack Ruby stepped in front of him, with the TV cameras filming live, and shot him. Oswald died later that day, at the same hospital where JFK did.

Jackie Kennedy suffered the devastating loss of her child and her husband within months of each other.

The attacks on Pearl Harbor on December 7, 1941, and on the twin towers in New York on September 11, 2001, are tragedies imprinted in the minds of this country. The assassination of President John F. Kennedy on November 22, 1963, forever altered our nation as well. "What was killed in Dallas," wrote *New York Times* columnist James Reston, "was not only the President but the promise." The events of that day, and the three days following Kennedy's assassination, became a series of images seared into the American memory—Jackie's bloodied pink suit, the riderless horse in JFK's funeral procession, the far-too-young children and grief-ravaged widow, John Jr. saluting his father's casket as it passed by. He had just turned three years old that day.

"All this will not be finished in the first one hundred days," Kennedy said in his inaugural address. "Nor will it be finished in the first one thousand days." And it wasn't—JFK was in office just 1,036 days. "But let us begin," he said. And the work

Afterward, the Warren Commission attempted to answer the question of "why." It is one that is, to this day, still asked.

he began—in civil rights, in the space mission, in creating programs and strengthening alliances throughout the world to protect democratic ideals—would continue for years to come. His legacy extends even beyond these policies to the spirit of high principles he inculcated in a nation, particularly its young people. In 1989, the Kennedy family established the Profile in Courage Award, named after JFK's Pulitzer Prize–winning book, honoring those who courageously follow their conscience without regard to personal consequence. Recipients of the Kennedy award include U.S. Representative Gabrielle "Gabby" Giffords and President Barack Obama.

On February 20, 2017, Presidents Day, the U.S. Post Office issued a stamp to commemorate the centenary of JFK's birth.

The final iconic image from Kennedy's funeral was the lighting of the Eternal Flame at his grave site in Arlington National Cemetery. The torch, to be forever lit, had been passed.